AMERICAN

IDIOTS

DR. GERALD H. SMITH

Copyright © 2023 Dr. Gerald H. Smith

ISBN 978-1-961227-16-3 (paperback)

ISBN 978-1-961227-17-0 (digital)

Digitally produced in the United States of America

American Idiot
- **Tragic story of the destruction of America**
- **Rampant political corruption**
- **How the Deep State has erected the Matrix**

Author: **Dr. Gerald H. Smith**

Editing by: **Dr. Gerald H. Smith**

Front cover design: **Johanna Bellerose**

All photographs taken by or obtained from the Internet: **Dr. Gerald H. Smith**

Main category: Non-fiction**: Corrupt political scene**

First Edition release date: January 1, 2023

Publisher: **ICNR Press**

303 Corporate Drive East • Langhorne, PA 19047

Web site: **www.icnr.com**

Preface

American Idiots was written in an attempt to wake up the normies who still have their heads in the sand. Unfortunately our mainstream media has brainwashed a large percentage of our population to the point where they can no longer think. Our great American republic is being torn apart by the Deep State players and even though people are experiencing the pain of this tragedy (increased gas and food prices, scarcity of consumer goods, mom and pop stores closing their doors forever, rampant unemployment, people sleeping on our streets, and many giving up their pets because they cannot afford to feed them) the American Idiots still show their "patriotism" by flying their flags stating they support Ukraine. In my humble opinion, I believe that once some of these American Idiots become awakened they will be unable to handle the psychological trauma that they have been duped. Mark Twain the great American satirist put it succinctly when he stated, "No amount of evidence will ever convince an idiot."

For those who are awake, I hope you can see some glimpses of humor within this great American tragedy that we are all immersed. As an optimist, I see daylight at the end of this perverted historical era that unfortunately must occur in order to recapture what our forefathers sacrificed so much to achieve. Mark Twain stated that if you do not read the newspaper you are uninformed and if you read the newspaper you are misinformed. CNN, MSNBC, and the rest of the mainstream media are sources disseminating disinformation and propaganda.

God Bless America and those patriots who are making the great sacrifice to turn around this run away train. Remember that our 1776 American Revolution was carried out by only 4% of the population.

Doctor Gerald Smith is a longtime holistic doctor, nutritionist, lecturer, and author with a thriving practice located in Bucks County, Pennsylvania. He is certified by the World Organization Of Natural Medicine to practice natural medicine globally. He is also a certified dental practitioner. His broad base of post-graduate training in dentistry and natural medicine enabled him to integrate many health care specialties. Sir, Doctor Smith is also a Knight Hospitaller a dedicated professional organization dating back to the year 1050. The Knights Hospitallers have official recognition from the United Nations and the Pope for their tremendous humanitarian work with the poor. For a full biography on Doctor Gerald Smith, please go to this site: https://icnr.com/about/

This is the eighth book authored by Doctor Gerald Smith. His previous two bestselling books were entitled, *Remove the "Splinters" and Watch the Body Heal* and *Cancer Deconstructed.*

Biggest American Idiot in the history of our republic is none other than the resident in the White House. Biden gets our **10 Pinocchio's rating.** You cannot make this shit up.

A direct quotation from the greatest American Idiot.

"We have put together the most extensive voter fraud organization in the history of American politics."

November 6, 2020

One of the Vice President's dumbest quotations.

"It is time for us to do what we have been doing and that time is every day." – Kamala Harris

So, it's time to keep doing NOTHING

Kamala Harris gets our 5 Pinocchio's rating.

"What do we know about this population, 18-24? They are stupid," "That is why we put them in dormitories and they have a resident assistant. They make really bad decisions."

Baby Fauci testified under oath before the United States Senate that the National Institutes of Health has not funded gain of function research in the Wuhan Institute of Virology yet a report by Project Veritas proves that baby Fauci did, in fact, fund research in Wuhan, China and at several sites across the United States.

Dr. Fauci has given contrary advice regarding the source of the virus, the transmissibility of the virus, the virulence of the virus, the efficacy of masks and "vaccines", the efficacy of social distancing, and has demeaned anyone in the public health community that disagrees with him. Dr. Fauci has continuously and deliberately misled the public at every turn. Fauci's continuos lying to the world gets our **10 Pinocchio's rating.**

Are you getting the "vaccine?" No, I'm waiting for the human trials to be completed. But Dr. Fauci said they were safe and if I keep my social distancing and wear a mask I won't get COVID.

Sadly, most people would gladly sacrifice freedom for the illusion of safety.

How do you get an entire choir to wear masks? Instill **Fear** and they will do anything you ask even though there is NO science to validate the demand. This gets our **Pinocchio rating of 6** for this scam.

Good old slick Willie: On Jan. 26, 1998 - Bill Clinton famously told the nation, "I did not have sexual relations with that woman, Miss Lewinsky." President Clinton gets our **Pinocchio rating of 10** for his big lie. The Lewinsky scandal remains the king of all American sex scandals.

Photo taken in the *oral* office

Alejandro Nicholas Mayorkas

Impeaching Alejandro Nicholas Mayorkas, seventh Secretary of Homeland Security, for high crimes and misdemeanors may now come true. He testified before the senate that our southwest borders are **safe and secure.** A top priority for DHS is to keep terrorists and their weapons from entering the U.S. while welcoming all legitimate travelers and commerce. DHS Officers and Agents **enforce all applicable U.S. laws, including against illegal immigration, narcotics smuggling, and illegal importation.** DHS deploys highly trained law enforcement personnel who apprehend more than 1,000 individuals each day for suspected violations of U.S. laws at and between our ports of entry. These immigrants are NOT vetted and NOT vaccinated! Mayorkas gets our **Pinocchio rating of 10.**

CLICK TO VIEW VIDEO

HON. ALEJANDRO MAYORKAS

BULLSHIT

AMERICA. THANK YOU VERY MUCH.

Crazy Nancy Pelosi ripping up a copy of President Trump's State of the Union Address before Congress. Only an idiot would disrespect the President of the United States before the whole world. Crazy Nancy gets our **Pinocchio rating** of **9** for her despicable behavior.

The six words that cost incumbent President George H.W. Bush to lose the 1992 Presidential Election to William Jefferson Clinton: **"Read my lips: No new taxes."** This big lie gets a **Pinocchio rating of 10.**

Just remember that the United States has the best two party dictatorship in the world. Both Bush and Clinton were both controlled by the Deep State.

Attorney General Eric Holder's Long History Of Lying To Congress

Fast and Furious was deliberately set up to fail by the Obama administration to pave the way for greater federal gun controls.

Holder's testimony before Congress:
"When did you first know about the program officially I believe called Fast and Furious? To the best of your knowledge, what date?" House Oversight Committee Chairman Darrell Issa asked Holder in sworn testimony on May 3, 2011. "I'm not sure of the exact date, but I probably heard about Fast and Furious for the first time over the last few weeks," was Holder's response.

Holder lied: A July 2010 memo shows Michael Walther, head of the National Drug Intelligence Center, told Holder that straw buyers in Fast and Furious "are responsible for the purchase of 1,500 firearms that were then supplied to the Mexican drug trafficking cartels."

House Judiciary Committee Chairman Lamar Smith, R-Texas, said other documents indicate Holder began receiving weekly briefings on the program from the National Drug Intelligence Center on or before that date.

And you wonder why the American people have lost confidence in our government especially when the Obama administration was trying to take away our second amendment. Holder gets our Pinocchio rating of 9.

Iran–Contra affair
1985–1987 political scandal in the U.S.

The Iran–Contra affair, often referred to as the Iran–Contra scandal was a political scandal in the United States that occurred during the second term of the Reagan administration. Between 1981 and 1986, senior administration officials secretly facilitated the sale of arms to Iran, which was the subject of an arms embargo. The administration hoped to use the proceeds of the arms sale to fund the Contras, a right-wing rebel group, in Nicaragua. Under the Boland Amendment, further funding of the Contras by the government had been prohibited by Congress.

The Iran–Contra affair is only the tip of the iceberg when it comes to the US funding of black operations and overthrowing third world country's regimes in order to put our puppets in power. Between 1947 and 1989, the U.S. tried to change other countries' governments 72 times during the Cold War. We give a **Pinocchio rating of 10** for all the lies disseminated via the mainstream media regarding our involvement in regime changes.

Article By John D. Morris special to The New York Times
Jan. 15, 1971

The Department of Transportation, in a special "consumer protection bulletin," warned owners of about 1.4 million Chevrolet Corvairs today of possible "health and safety hazards" (carbon monoxide leaking into the car's cabin) in the heating systems of their cars.

Mr. Nader called on the Secretary of Transportation, John A. Volpe, to require the company to notify Corvair owners of a safety defect in their heaters. The Safety Administration took the position today that it did not have sufficient evidence to order a defect notification by General Motors but said it was "now turning its attention to an intensive survey of a random sampling of Corvair vehicles."

General Motors issued a statement disavowing any inherent defect in Corvair heaters. Leakage of objectionable fumes from the heating system into the passenger area would not occur, the company said, "if the vehicle is properly maintained and in good working order."

Do you still believe your government and car manufacturers are looking out for your best interests? This egregious cover-up gets our **Pinocchio rating of 10.**

How are Flame Retardant Chemicals in Pajamas Dangerous?

The harm in the 70s was from brominated tris, which could damage DNA, then chlorinated tris, which also was found to mutate DNA. (That one is still in use today in infant products and furniture, just not PJs!) Lovely.

Newer flame retardants called PBDEs may cause "thyroid disruption, memory and learning problems, delayed mental and physical development, lower IQ, advanced puberty and reduced fertility."

PBDE was finally banned in 2005, but they're in so many products still in homes, like couches, mattresses, carpet pads, and children's items like changing table pads.

It seems every flame retardant chemical used widely thus far has ended up being banned because it was so dangerous, and most if not all of the chemicals still used to make furniture and carpet flame-resistant have major health risks.

"Since tris flame retardants were removed from children's pajamas in the 1970s, more than 3,000 peer-reviewed studies have documented the ability of similar classes of flame retardants to accumulate or to harm health.

We have more than enough research data to support not putting such potentially harmful compounds in furniture and other consumer products. We give this industry a **Pinocchio rating of 10** because of their lack of concern for children's safety. What would you rather risk: a small, open flame, or 12 hours of exposure to a likely toxic chemical every single night for your kids?

How to discern medical propaganda? It's very simple. Be aware of the words they use to character assassinate the inventor or originator of any discovery. What's their agenda. Their agenda is simple. To prevent their revenue stream from being shut off. When you read such words like unscientific, not validated, or pseudoscience you can be sure the powers to be are on the attack. One such discovery that was suppressed in the 1920s, was the compound, glyoxylide, discovered by Dr. William F. Koch. Dr. Koch had impeccable medical credentials. He discovered that glyoxylide was present in the human brain and was effective in suppressing cancer. When this compound was injected into cancer patients who were on their death bed, many were cured in seven to ten days. The reason the medical cartel trashed Dr. Koch and labeled him a quack was because he would not give the big boys his formula so they could rape the population. You can read more about his discovery at **www.williamfkoch.com**. This was one of the greatest cancer discoveries and losses in medical history. But the medical establishment doesn't really care about you. You can read more about natural cancer discoveries in the book, *Politics in Healing*, by Daniel Haley. Eleven other major cancer cures were also squashed. The so called War on Cancer was a total failure and used to pump over 500 billion dollars into the academic welfare system. The idiots that destroyed this discovery should be hanged. We give these American Idiots a **10 Pinocchio rating** because of all the lives that could have been saved and the suffering that could have been avoided.

William F. Koch (1885-1967)c

Stanley Meyer's Car that runs on water

The water fuel cell is a technical design of a "perpetual motion machine" created by American Stanley Allen Meyer (August 24, 1940 – March 20, 1998). Meyer claimed that an automobile retrofitted with the device could use water as fuel instead of gasoline. Meyer's claims about his "Water Fuel Cell" and the car that it powered were found to be fraudulent by an Ohio court in 1996. Watch the video and judge for yourself.

Another example of suppression of technology and inventor character assassination. Stan Meyer drove his water fueled car across the US. If such an invention was unfounded, why was Stan murdered? The reason is simple. Such a device would dramatically reduce the revenue stream of the oil industry. We give oil industry idiots a **Pinocchio rating of 9** for their greed and disregard for humanity.

Global Warming Hoax

Pinocchio Rating of 10 for Gore's bad bullshit

One of America's biggest hoaxsters is Al Gore. His global warming theory is just that a theory. Through the years his global warming fear mongering turned into the rhetoric that we are going to have a global ice age. Now the American idiot is using a generic label, Climate Change. Climate campaigns in the 1970s were warning us of flooding and loss of coastal property to occur by the year 2000. It is very interesting that the so called "elite" have been buying water front properties (Nancy Pelosi and Obama to name a few). Gore's agenda along with the other idiots was to establish a carbon tax for all nations so the "elite" could steal billions of dollars from the fund. The following information is presented for those who still buy into the climate hoax.

A letter signed by over 50 leading members of the American Meteorological Society warned about the policies promoted by environmental **pressure groups.** "The policy initiatives derive from **highly uncertain scientific theories.** They are based on the **unsupported assumption** that catastrophic global warming follows from the burning of fossil fuel and requires immediate action. We do not agree." Those who have signed the letter represent the overwhelming majority of climate change scientists in the United States, of whom there are about 60. McMichael and Haines quote the 1995 report of the Intergovernmental Panel on Climate Change (IPCC), which is widely believed to "prove" that climate change induced by humans has occurred. The original draft document did not say this. What happened was that the policymakers' summary (which became the "take home message" for politicians) **altered the conclusions of the scientists.** This led Dr. Frederick Seitz, former head of the United States National Academy of Sciences, to write, "In more than sixty years as a member of the American scientific community ... **I have never witnessed a more disturbing corruption of the peer-review process than the events that led to this IPCC report.**"

1. **Michaels P.** Conspiracy, consensus or correlation? What scientists think about the 'popular vision' of global warming. World Climate Review. 1993;1:11. [Google Scholar]
2. **McMichael AJ, Haines A.** Global climate change: the potential effects on health. BMJ. 1997;315:805–809. [PMC free article] [PubMed] [Google Scholar]
3. **Seitz F.** Major deception on global warning. Wall Street Journal 1996 June 12;section A:16(col 3).
4. **Balling RC.** Global warming: messy models, decent data and pointless policy. **In:**
5. **Bailey R, editor.** The true state of the planet. New York: Free Press; 1995. pp. 83–107. [Google Scholar]

Gov. Gavin Newsom: Typical American Political Idiot Puppet

When every body was being forced to abide by COVID restrictions (masks, 6 foot distancing, etc.), the arrogant Gov. of California, Gavin Newsom attended a party at the posh French Laundry restaurant in Los Angeles without a mask or social distancing. Gov. Newsom was a student of the self appointed "global leader" Klaus Schwab of the Economic Forum who said that by 2030 we will all own nothing and be happy. Newsom is also the nephew of Nancy Pelosi and was embedded as Gov. of California to destroy its economy. We assign the illustrious idiot puppet a Pinocchio rating of 9 for his deceitful and destructive mandates.

Another well deserved bullshit award for a political hack.

Tip of the Hillary Clinton Corrupt and Treasonous Iceberg

When Hillary lost her bid for presidency in the rigged 2016 election in which the Dominion voting machines were manipulated for her to win, she was reported to be cursing like a truck driver.

Federal Election Commission (FEC) fines Hillary Clinton campaign and DNC over Trump-Russia dossier research. The DNC was fined $105,000 and the Clinton campaign was fined $8,000, according to a letter sent by the Federal Election Commission to a conservative group that requested an inquiry. Political candidates and groups are required to publicly disclose their spending to the FEC, and they must explain the purpose of any specific expenditure more than $200. The FEC concluded that the Clinton campaign and DNC misreported the money that funded the dossier, masking it as "legal services" and "legal and compliance consulting" instead of opposition research.

The dossier was compiled by retired British spy Christopher Steele. It contained **unverified and salacious allegations** about Donald Trump, including claims that his campaign colluded with the Kremlin to win the 2016 election. Trump's campaign had numerous contacts with Russian agents, and embraced Russian help, but no one was ever formally accused of conspiring with Russia.

The money trail behind the Steele dossier has been a subject of intense political scrutiny for years. More than $1 million flowed from the Clinton campaign and DNC to the law firm Perkins Coie, which then hired the opposition research company Fusion GPS. That company later hired Steele and asked him to use his overseas contacts to dig up dirt about Trump's ties to Russia. Special prosecutor, Attorney Robert Durham, in his recent indictments proved without a shadow of a doubt that the Steel dossier was totally fictitious; that the FBI, DOJ and other governmental agencies lied about the Steele dossier and covered-up the fact that the dossier was fake, phony, and false. Spying on a sitting president is an act of treason. The Clinton's are another example of corrupt politicians who have sold their soul to the highest bidder. We give Hitlary the coveted **Pinocchio rating of 10** for her treasonous acts.

FYI Hillary Clinton's non-profit Foundation, received a donation of 145 million dollars for her green lighting the Uranium One deal when she was Secretary of State; Rosatom mining company, backed by the Russian state, acquired a Canadian uranium mining company, now called Uranium One, which has assets in the U.S. Uranium is a key material for making nuclear weapons. Could this be construed as an act of treason?

How False Intel and a Massive U.S. Propaganda Machine Bolstered Baby George W. Bush's War on Iraq

It was the "decision of one man to launch a wholly unjustified and brutal invasion of Iraq in 2003," which was based on false intelligence reports and the mantra of "Weapons of Mass Destruction" (watch the movie Green Zone). "How many Americans, Iraqis and others have died (over 1 million) and be crippled by him for a lie? Bush's brother Jeb, in a 2015 presidential debate, when asked by moderator Megyn Kelly whether "your brother's war was a mistake," said the invasion was wrong and based on "faulty intelligence."

Raw intelligence is overrated. Although it has been reported that Baby Bush was smart in private, he was still a very bad president. Presidential scholars rank him 38th on the list. He left office with dismal approval ratings.

For crimes against humanity, we bestow a **Pinocchio rating of 10** for his unjust war, 911 inside job (Richard Gage: youtube.com/watch?v=-NZwPqXRu_I), and 2008 dangerous free fall of the economy that led to controversial and expensive government intervention in financial markets. In a Pew Research poll, only 13% said Bush made progress toward solving the major issues facing the country.

How Jane Fonda's 1972 trip to North Vietnam earned her the nickname 'Hanoi Jane'

There is an old saying that there are no victims only volunteers. Unfortunately, we may never get the real truth about the incident when "Hanoi Jane" had her picture taken with North Vietnamese soldiers on an anti-aircraft gun in North Vietnam. The activist later stated that she was lured into the situation without thinking of the consequences of her action. Fonda was committed to ending the war and her

extreme commitment clouded her thinking. Images are very powerful and this one stuck in the minds of many people who cannot forgive her action. Fonda said she didn't realize at the time the effect posing with the anti-aircraft gun would have. "I know the power of images," she said in an 1988 interview on ABCs "20-20." "To have put myself in a situation like that was a thoughtless and cruel thing to have done. ... I take full responsibility for it." We all have made mistakes in our lives but most if not all were never photographed. Because of the circumstances surrounding her behavior we are bypassing any Pinocchio rating. I believe that the pain "Hanoi Jane" has endured is punishment enough.

Someone once said, "to forgive is wisdom, to forget is genius."

Alexandria Ocasio-Cortez

Alexandria Ocasio-Cortez, also known by her initials AOC, is an American politician and activist. She has served as the U.S. representative for New York's 14th congressional district since 2019, as a member of the Democratic Party.

"As a politician she has accomplished nothing and has not lifted a finger on behalf of this country." AOC is a drama queen and is as dumb as they come. She was successful in diverting Amazon from establishing a distribution warehouse in NY and successfully orchestrated the loss of 18,000 jobs for New Yorkers. AOC has a big mouth but never once has agreed to be interviewed by any one of substance." The key to this idiots political success is that our population has been dumb down so much that many people cannot think and analyze what she is saying. Our country is in a sad state of affairs and partly due to idiots like AOC. The dumbocrats are destroying our southern border and immigration, they are trying to destroy our electoral college, they want to "fix" the supreme court by expanding it, they are trying to destroy the states voting systems, they have no blueprint for alternative energy, they have shut off our energy supply, they have destroyed women's sports, they are destroying our monetary system by creating trillions of dollars out of thin air, they are trying to start World War III to cover their reset to a digital monetary and communist social system, they have no idea how the private sector works, they want to compel abortion all over the country, and if you do not agree with them they will try to destroy you by calling you a white supremacist. Hands down, AOC is awarded our highest **Pinocchio rating of 10+.**

Yes my IQ is Zero; that's why I advocate that the student loans should be paid off by the taxpayers.

Lance Armstrong

Lance Armstrong, a former American road-racing cyclist, helped elevate cycling to global popularity. His seven consecutive Tour de France victories, from 1999 to 2005, and his status as a cancer survivor made him one of the most iconic and revered athletes outside of the professional sports world.

The Lance Armstrong doping case was a major doping investigation that led to retired American road racing cyclist Lance Armstrong being stripped of his seven consecutive Tour de France titles, along with one Olympic medal, and his eventual admission to using performance-enhancing drugs. The United States Anti-Doping Agency (USADA) portrayed Armstrong as the ringleader of what it called "the most sophisticated, professionalized and successful doping program that sport has ever seen."

In a January interview with Oprah Winfrey, Armstrong finally admits to doping during each Tour de France win from 1999 to 2005.

"This story was so perfect for so long. It's this myth, this perfect story, and it wasn't true," Armstrong tells Winfrey.

"I viewed this situation as one big lie that I repeated a lot of times, and as you said, it wasn't as if I just said no and I moved off it."

Armstrong was arrogant and unfortunately helped destroy many professional careers along the way. For those who do not believe in karma, you better rethink your belief system.

Karma

- Armstrong announces he is stepping down as chairman of Livestrong.
- Nike terminates its contract with Lance Armstrong.
- Anheuser-Busch also announces it will not renew its contract with Armstrong after it expires in 2012.
- UCI strips Armstrong of his seven Tour de France titles and bans him for life.
- Oakley announces it is severing ties with Armstrong.
- The Justice Department files a lawsuit against Armstrong and his company Tailwind Sports for millions of dollars that the US Postal Service spent to sponsor his team. The complaint charges that the use of prohibited drugs constitutes a breach of contract.

Although Armstrong's accomplishments were great, cheating brought all his glory to a screeching halt. We give lance a **Pinocchio rating of 10.** As a cyclist myself, I watched all his Tour de France races, which all turned out to be an illusion.

"Of all the animals, man is the only one that lies."

Mark Twain

How to spot an American idiot. Any time you see a car with a bumper sticker that says I or we support Ukraine or a lawn sign that says we support Ukraine you know that these people have bought into the mainstream propaganda that Putin attacked the country to annex it. The truth of the matter is that Putin went into Ukraine for three primary reasons:

1. To eliminate the 31 bio labs that were funded by the United States to develop and disseminate biological warfare.
2. To eliminate the worlds' biggest money laundering country that was being used to launder funds and sending them back to Obama, Clintons, the Biden crime family and the democratic party.
3. Ukraine was one of the major child and women trafficking countries in the world.

A little history will set the stage for a better understanding of what is really going on in Ukraine. The first duly elected president of Ukraine was Leonid Makarovych Kravchuk. Unfortunately, Obama had him removed in 1991 by a rigged election and they put in the puppet, Zelenskyy. Also the special military group of the CIA stole 33 tons of gold from the Ukraine treasury.

These issues were never presented to the American public and the propaganda being spun out to the public is a mind control technique to distract people from the truth. Also the Deep State is trying to depose Putin because he is not on board with the climate change hoax, has plenty of oil and natural gas, and a stable currency.

Jen Psaki's disinformation, lies, smears, and idiocy

Jen Psaki made some terse remarks at the Fox news journalist Peter Doocy. Her statement, "is he a stupid son of a b**** or does he play a stupid son of a b**** on TV were all designed to distract people from Doocy's many poignant probing questions regarding President Biden's shutting down the Keystone pipeline, his inflation policies, his bungling of the Afghanistan pull out, his open southern border policy, not vetting the illegal immigrants entering the US, and many more topics that apparently irritated the White House press secretary. As with all Marxist playbook tactics, always attack your opponent and blame them with the same actions that you are doing.

I told you inflation was only transient. You can cut your gas bill in half at the pump if you just fill your tank when it is half empty! You can immediately save 50%! Because Jen Psaki is only a pawn in this political chess game and told what to say, we only bestowed a **Pinocchio rating of 4.**

Typical Mainstream Media Propaganda and Lies

Hitler's minister of propaganda, Joseph Goebbles, always said, that if you tell a big enough lie long enough people will believe it.

Twice-impeached former President Donald Trump blasted out a brief statement on Saturday night that appeared to unintentionally refute his own long-running (and bogus) claim that the 2020 election was stolen from him. "Anybody that doesn't think there wasn't massive Election Fraud in the 2020 Presidential Election is either very stupid, or very corrupt!" the statement read.

Trump's (apparently) accidental double-negative means the opposite of what Trump and numerous conservatives have been falsely insisting about the 2020 presidential outcome. During the end of his presidency, Trump led a failed, anti-democratic, and at times deadly GOP crusade, based on baseless claims of election fraud, to try and overturn Joe Biden's 2020 victory. Trump and various figures in the Republican Party have continued pushing these lies in their efforts to execute an increasing number of election and voting crackdowns across the country.

My answer to the mainstream media's fake, phony, and false, statements about the 2020 election is to present a direct quotation by Joe Biden made on November 6, 2020: "We have put together the most extensive voter fraud organization in the history of American politics." Case closed.

If you want additional validation watch the documentary 2000 Mules; when you do not have all the facts, it is easy for one to be mind controlled and accept the fake new 's statements about the 2020 election. For more validation that our election process has been hijacked, one just has to view what took place in the 2022 Mid-Term elections. Voting machines were not working in Maricopa County Arizona, Mercer County New Jersey and many other republican strong holds through out the country. Printing machines ran out of ink and now we have election month because the democrats need more time to produce more ballots to win. The democratic machine gets our **Pinocchio rating of 8** for their blatant cheating efforts.

Sheep Being Led to Slaughter

How does one create a pandemic. First you create the **FEAR** of an unknown villain like a virus. Then you get the mainstream media to hype it up. Then you need to validate the wide spread hysteria by driving up the number of cases. How does one accomplish that. Easy. You develop a test that falsely creates positive results. That's exactly what they did with the PCR test. The inventor of PCR test, Dr. Kary B. Mullis, never said it was designed to detect infectious diseases. But the powers to be didn't care of its accuracy. All they needed was a test to convince people they had COVID.

At the media briefing on COVID-19 on March 16, 2020, the WHO Director General Dr. Tedros Adhanom Ghebreyesus said:

We have a simple message for all countries: test, test, test."

The message was spread through headlines around the world, for instance by Reuters and the BBC.

Still on the 3 of May, the moderator of the heute journal — one of the most important news magazines on German television— was passing the mantra of the corona dogma on to his audience with the admonishing words:

Test, test, test—that is the credo at the moment, and it is the only way to really understand how much the coronavirus is spreading."

This indicates that the belief in the validity of the PCR tests is so strong that it equals a religion that tolerates virtually **no contradiction.**

Now that you have the population at large all scared out of their minds you need free testing centers. Once someone is labeled COVID positive it's easy to get them take the jab.

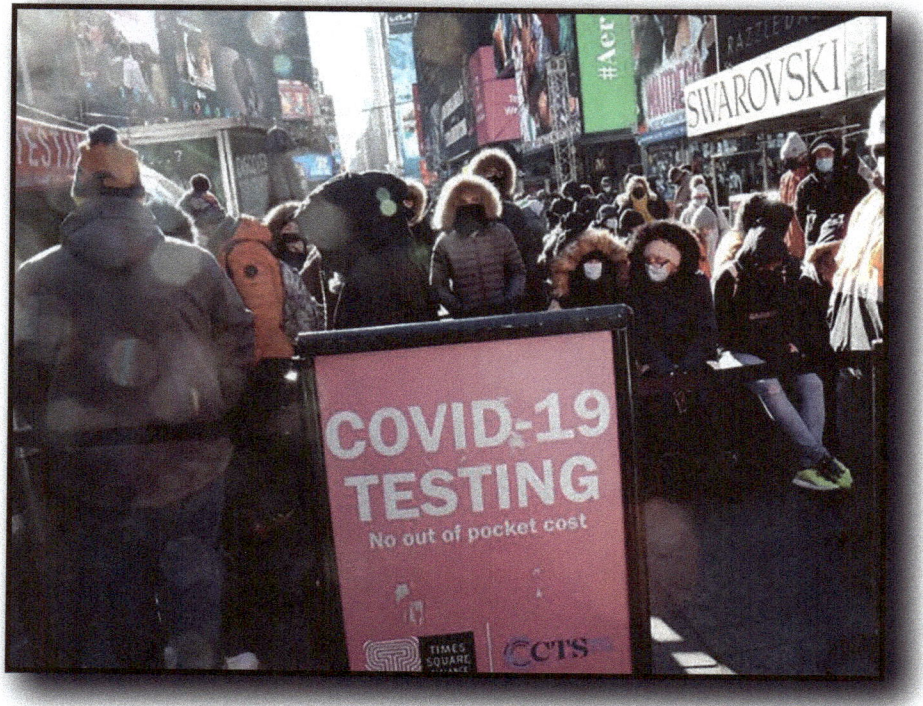

People face long lines as they rush to get tested for COVID ahead of the holidays.

If the PCR test is so good and valid, why did the FDA terminate its use on December 31, 2021? Because it is not accurate. We have to give these criminals a **Pinocchio rating of 9** for there efficient mind control tactics to whip up hysteria.

Dr. Kary Mullis passed away in 2021 at the age of 74, but there is no doubt that the biochemist regarded the PCR test as inappropriate to detect a viral infection.

"It is easier to fool people than convince them that they have been fooled."

Mark Twain

Fish Oil Scam

Problem reaction solution is a Hegelian Dialectic. It's philosophy is used as an interpretive method in which the contradiction between a proposition (thesis) and its antithesis is resolved at a higher level of truth (synthesis). You create a problem: cardiovascular issues like heart attacks. The establishment already knows the reaction FEAR. Please save us from having a heart attack. The knight rides in on his big white horse with the solution: **Fish oil.** The pharmaceutical companies have spent millions of dollars and ten years to brainwash the dumbed down doctors to prescribe fish oil. In fact, fish oil is the most prescribed supplement on the market today.

Now comes the bad news. Fish oil at body temperature becomes **RANCID! This is why you belch and burp and your stomach does not feel so good when you take the rancid oil.** Don't take my word for it. Read Prof. Brian S. Peskin's book, *PEO Solution*. He gives 10 inconvenient truths (pp. 243 - 248) with the scientific citations of the studies about fish oil. Fish oil is physiologically wrong for humans!

1. It fails to prevent either primary or secondary cardio vascular disease.
2. It increases the endothelial lining of the blood vessels causing platelet adhesion in heart patients.
3. DHA and fish oil are shown as completely worthless in the treatment for Alzheimer's.
4. Fish oil increases the risk of colon cancer.
5. Blood sugar control worsens during fish oil administration.
6. Fish oil ruins mitochondria (energy producing organelles within a cell) functionality.
7. Fish oil accelerates aging by increasing oxidative stress.
8. Fish oil does not slow atherosclerosis in patients with existing arterial disease.
9. Fish oil continues to fail in preventing cancer.
10. Fish oil adversely affects chemotherapy.

The real solution is taking organic, cold pressed omega 6 and omega 3 oils. Why. Because the adulterated omega 6 oils that we all get in our diets causes our cell membranes to literally turn to plastic. This is why one gets diabetes. You become insulin resistant. Your cell membranes are chemically like plastic and resistant to the insulin bringing in the glucose. Omega 6 oils (safflower, sunflower, avocado, walnut oil) repairs the damaged plastic membrane and acts as a magnet bringing oxygen into the cell. Omega 6 oils are anti-inflammatory contrary to what your doctor tells you. All the studies carried out with omega 6 oils were done with adulterated omega 6, which is pro-inflammatory. In addition omega 6 oils are Parent Essential Oils, that is, they can convert into any oil the body needs. Peskin's research shows that the skin has a 1000:1 ratio of omega 6 to omega 3; the nervous system has a 100:1 ratio of omega 6 to omega 3; the organs have a 4.5:1 omega 6 to omega 3; the adipose tissue (fat) has a 22.5:1 ration of omega 6 to omega 3. How can omega 3s be more important than omega6s? Unfortunately, most doctors are 20 years behind the present scientific literature. A **Pinocchio rating of 8** is awarded to the pharmaceutical companies big fish oil scam.

Dead Doctors Don't Lie

Dr. Joel Wallach wrote the book, *Dead Doctors Don't Lie,* to drive home the point that most physicians are NOT healthy themselves. In fact, when he traveled around the country, he made it a point to check the obituaries. He noticed a very peculiar common denominator, that is, most doctors listed had an average age of death of 54 years-old. Are you really going to trust these quacks who can't even keep themselves healthy to treat you?

Dr. Wallach discovered that many of the doctors did, in fact, die much younger than the national average, and this was because they "practiced what they preached," or took the drugs they prescribed, to numb the pain rather than cure the problem. Interestingly, he maintained that every death was actually attributable to a mineral deficiency, even though that was not the apparent cause of death. The information put forth may be the stimulus you need to change your lifestyle. We bestow a **Pinocchio rating of 6** to all those dead doctors who were led down the illusory allopathic path of healing.

God Bless America

What is this country coming to?

It has been said that God made men and women and democrats made all other genders. Please meet our new assistant secretary of health, Doctor Rachel Levine. So Rachel how long have you been a woman?

American Standard has a whole new line of transgender urinals.

What constitutes inciting a riot?

Maxine Waters (D-Los Angeles) while in Brooklyn Center, Minn., protesting the police shooting death of Daunte Wright, appeared to tell protesters that they needed to get "more confrontational" if the jury in the Derek Chauvin trial does not return a guilty verdict. If Donald Trump made this statement he would have been indicted for instigating an insurrection. Why is it that only conservatives get bad press, indictments, subpoenas, and smeared by the press? We give a **Pinocchio rating of 7** for her statement to spur a crowd on to get "more confrontational."

Representative Maxine Waters(C) (D-CA) speaks to the media during an ongoing protest at the Brooklyn Center Police Department in Brooklyn Centre, Minnesota on April 17, 2021. - Police officer, Kim Potter, who shot dead Black 20-year-old Daunte Wright in a Minneapolis suburb after appearing to mistake her gun for her Taser was arrested April 14 on manslaughter charges.

Fox News Bill O'Reilly gets slammed for his off color remarks about Maxine Water's hair

A genius is someone who recognizes the obvious. This appears to be the case with Bill O'Reilly's comment regarding Maxine Water's hair. O'Reilly's comment came during a segment on the network's morning show, in which Mr. O'Reilly was shown observing a speech by Ms. Waters, a frequent critic of President Trump. When asked for his thoughts, Mr. O'Reilly said, "I didn't hear a word she said. I was looking at the James Brown wig."

Mr. O'Reilly's quips received widespread denunciations as the segment spread on social media, with some attacking them as racially charged. Mr. O'Reilly issued a written statement: "As I have said many times, I respect Congresswoman Maxine Waters for being sincere in her beliefs. I said that again today on 'Fox and Friends' calling her 'old school.' Unfortunately, I also made a jest about her hair which was dumb. I apologize." He repeated the apology on his show, though inadvertently calling her a "congressman."

James Brown the Godfather of Soul

Free fall or demolition? You be the judge

The National Institute of Standards and Technology's (NIST) report stated that the collapse of World trade Center Building 7 collapsed due to raging fires. History documents that no tall building ever collapsed primarily due to fire. In a side-by-side video comparison, Building 7's collapse looks exactly like a building being demolished. You be the judge.

You do not have to be a rocket scientist to see the similarities. One of Building 7's tenants was a secret CIA office; rumors have been circulating that they had many of the reports regarding the JFK assassination. There is also rumors that all the Enron records were also housed in Building 7. Will we ever find out the truth? My instinct is that the Deep State does not want this information to see the light of day. The destruction of the Twin Towers and Building 7 could be one of the biggest inside jobs every pulled by any government. We give these NIST report, and the criminals who pulled off this heinous crime a **Pinocchio rating of 10.**

The Big Lie: COVID "vaccination" confers superior protection compared to the natural immunity.

One of the most egregious nullifications of medical scientific truth is the claim that COVID "vaccination" confers superior protection compared to the natural immunity you get after you've been exposed to the virus and recover. The reality is that natural immunity is infinitely more superior to the vaccine-induced protection you get from these shots, which is both narrow and temporary. **Our Surgeon General is lying to the people by telling them that natural immunity doesn't work.** Even the FDA is saying that there is NO natural immunity. Just not so.

When mainstream media, your dumb down doctor, FDA, CDC, your own government Surgeon General all tell the same big lie, you start to believe it. The COVID shot produces antibodies against just one of the viral proteins, the spike protein, whereas natural immunity produces antibodies against all parts of the virus, plus memory T cells.

Johns Hopkins studies show strength and duration of natural immunity protection. Natural immunity was six times stronger during the Delta wave than vaccination, according to one news report about the CDC study.

A new study from Israel, which is yet to be peer reviewed, concluded that natural immunity confers longer-lasting and stronger protection against infection, symptomatic disease and hospitalization caused by the Delta variant of SARS-CoV-2, compared with immunity induced from two doses of the Pfizer-BioNTech two-dose vaccine.

Natural infection exposes the immune system to a wider range of viral material and several viral proteins, the vaccines give a more targeted response to parts of the spike protein only and in this regard are more restricted.

Don't be fooled by the propaganda of mainstream media, FDA, CDC, and your doctor. We give the ABC organizations a **Pinocchio rating of 6.**
Louisiana Attorney General Alleges Fauci and Big Tech Part of Push to Censor Americans' Speech.

We are experiencing the same situation that Nazi Germany did in the early 1930s when free speech began to be taken away. It's like cooking a frog. If you turn up the heat slowly the frog will stay in the pot until it dies.

Trumps' 2016 win over Hillary Clinton derailed the Deep States' 16 year plan to take over the US and subvert our freedoms. They are four years behind schedule because of Trump's win. This is the reason they have ramped up their efforts.

"Louisiana Attorney General Jeff Landry and Missouri's Attorney General Eric Schmitt in May sued Anthony Fauci, the Biden administration, the Centers for Disease Control and Prevention (CDC), the Department of Homeland Security (DHS), and the FBI, alleging they censored American's free speech on social media platforms.

"Basically, when Anthony Fauci spoke, Americans were censored by Big Tech." Landry added that thanks to the First Amendment, the U.S. government is prohibited from censoring people's speech. He said that same amendment also prevents the government from telling companies to censor speech on their behalf.

Landry further alleged that government cooperation isn't limited to the COVID-19 pandemic. It's instead happening in many instances and gave the example of what he claimed was a media and government cover up of the Hunter Biden laptop story.

In June, Sen. Chuck Grassley (R-Iowa) released a letter he sent to Homeland Security Secretary Alejandro Mayorkas.

The letter stated that despite Department of Homeland Security's claims to the contrary, "documents show that the Disinformation Governance Board (DGB) was designed to be the department's central hub, clearinghouse, and gatekeeper for administration policy and response to whatever it happened to decide was 'disinformation.'"

Landry stated that the government's attempt to establish the DGB is a perfect example of what's going wrong in America.

"This is where the government is going out there and censoring Americans' ability to speak to one another on social platforms. [The U.S. government is] utilizing the social platform in a way to manipulate the American public into a one-size fits all policy."

Landry stated, "I can tell you this; this lawsuit is not going away. We intend to take this to trial." (This information was quoted from a recent Epoch Times article by Katie Spence December 1, 2022)

If "We the People" do not push back, it will be all over for America. Wake up normies.

The "Big Guy" is directed by the Deep State puppet masters what to sign, what to say and do. America is being run by a "president" who has dementia and is a paid hack was installed to destroy the United States. We are the laughing stock of the world. We bestow a **Pinocchio rating of 9** to the Biden Administration for their attempt to suppress our First Amendment Rights in an attempt to turn America into a socialist/communist state.

The January 6 Unselect Committee Represents One of the Biggest Travesties in American History

The January 6, 2022 event when Ex-President Donald J. Trump spoke in Washington, DC was set up to discrete the former 45th President and falsely claim he incited a riot. The truth is that crazy Nancy Pelosi orchestrated the "insurrection" by failing to provide National Guard security and utilizing FBI provocateurs to insight a staged "insurrection." Many of the Trump supporters who were incarcerated are still in jail and have NOT been charged with any crimes. This is totally unconstitutional and a major violation of these peoples' rights.

House Speaker Nancy Pelosi is being criticized for hiding her role in the security breakdowns on Jan. 6, and some allegations say she may be culpable for the chaos. Republicans are trying to obtain documents on Pelosi's role on the day, and claim their efforts are being blocked. In addition, there are over 14,000 hours of security tapes that Nancy Pelosi will NOT release. This democrat run administration has total disregard for any laws, the Constitution, and human rights. Their ultimate agenda is an attempt to indict former President Trump to prevent him from running in the 2024 election.

When "President" Biden was asked if he runs for president in the 2024 election what will be his slogan. He quickly stated, if I become president in 2024 you will freeze for freedom. We award the highest **Pinocchio rating of 10** for the outrageous corruption carried out by crazy Nancy Pelosi and the Biden administration. Must watch documentary, **The Real Story of Jan 6** (on Epoch Times website). This is being touted as the New Benghazi.

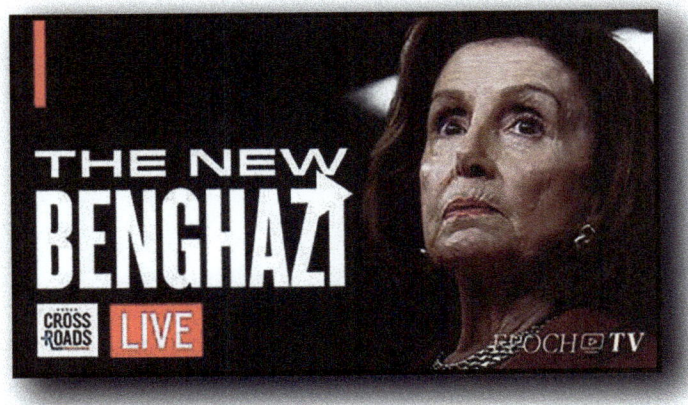

Marxist Playbook: Accuse your Opposition of the Exact Same Tactic You are Carrying Out!

The disinformation that was and is being put out by Ex-President Barak Obama and the resident Joe Biden represents the Marxist playbook tactics to distract people from the truth. These criminals have a well funded and well orchestrated assault on democracy and freedom of speech and are the best propagandists money can buy. The scientific documentation coming out now shows the horrific side effects and devistation that the COVID Franken shot is wreaking on people across the globe. Once people who got the poisonous shot wake up, they are going to be enraged. If the "COVID vaccines" are so safe and effective, why is the Red Cross refusing to accept blood donors from the vaccinated?

The narrative presented by the above criminals is pure propaganda and an attempt to dissuade people from hearing the truth. The short video clip below gives you a small sampling of the damage being caused by the jab. For more information, watch the video at https://braveseries.com/episode-4-live/.

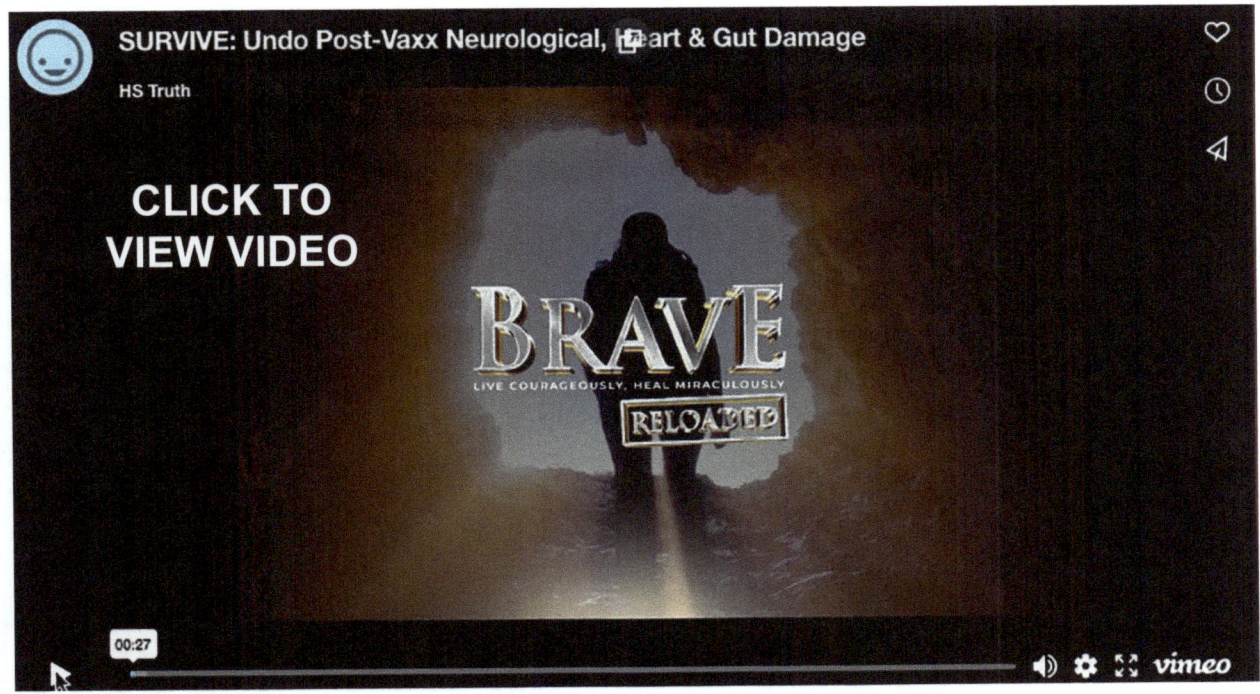

CDC Study confirms COVID Vaccination increases risk of suffering Autoimmune Disease affecting Heart by 13,200%

Myocarditis Cases Reported After mRNA-Based COVID-19 Vaccination in the US From December 2020 to August 2021
Matthew E. Oster, MD, MPH1,2,3; David K. Shay, MD, MPH1; John R. Su, MD, PhD, MPH1; et al. JAMA Jan. 25, 2022.

How to Spot American Idiots: Those wearing masks

The facts are simple. The virus is one micron in size and the pores in the mask are 80 microns in size. You do the math. There are over 170 peer reviewed scientific medical studies that document that masks do **NOT** work; also wearing a mask increases bacterial contamination and increases your chances of getting a respiratory infection; plus six foot social distancing also does not work. In addition, what these idiots do not realize is that they are breathing in fibers from these cheap masks which are affecting their lungs. Of further note, masks decrease your oxygen levels and raise your CO_2 levels. Children forced to wear masks in school has the potential of preventing normal brain development. Despite all the science there are plenty of idiots that still wear their masks while driving alone, jogging in fresh air, or playing golf. It's all based on **FEAR**. My question to all these idiots is do you wear your mask while having sex?

"No amount of evidence will ever persuade an idiot." Mark Twain

The Evil Of The Political Left Is Rooted In Their Exploitation Of Tragedies

by Brandon Smith | Alt-Market.us

November 30th 2022,

This article is so well written, I had to present the entire piece for fear of loosing the impact of what it had to say.

"What is the root of all evil? Money? No, not really. Money is just a tool, like a hammer, a wrench or even a gun. When I think of evil I don't envision a handgun or a rifle or a big pile of hundred dollar bills. Instead, I see nightly news talking heads spreading disinformation and fear. I see mobs of over-emotional and ignorant activists setting fire to buildings, tearing things down because they don't know how to build anything useful and new. And above it all, I see a small group of elites hovering, licking their chops as they fantasize about the potential power that can be gained from exploiting the chaos."

"The willingness to destroy and cause suffering for personal benefit is evil. The willingness to feed off the tragedies of others is evil. And these are the cold characteristics that currently define the political left."

"There have been multiple criminal events and national emergencies over the past few years that leftists have been very quick to hijack or scapegoat onto conservatives, often with embarrassing results for themselves. The most recent being the Colorado "Club Q" shooting in which 5 people died and at least 19 were injured. Here was the mainstream media's reaction to the event, with little to no facts on hand to back their claims:"

You can view the video on: https://www.infowars.com/posts/the-evil-of-the-political-left-is-rooted-in-their-exploitation-of-tragedies/

"Leftists use a very predictable strategy when it comes to these kinds of high profile criminal acts – Immediately blame all conservatives and conservative principles for the crimes of one man. Even if the event had nothing to do with conservatives, let the public think it did. If a gun is involved, blame the legality of guns in general as if the weapon is the problem rather than the mental illness or psychopathy of the perpetrator."

"As it turns out, the Club Q shooter suspect, Anderson Aldrich, is actually a member of the LGBT community and identifies as non-binary with They/Them pronouns. Watch this CNN anchor's response as she is forced to admit on air that the suspect does not fit CNN's original narrative:"

You can view the video on: https://www.infowars.com/posts/the-evil-of-the-political-left-is-rooted-in-their-exploitation-of-tragedies/

"She is clearly upset and bewildered at the revelation, and the guests even start making excuses, suggesting that perhaps the suspect is lying about his gender identity (which is rather ironic). But why did they react this way? Aren't they supposed to be objective journalists merely reporting the facts as they become available? Yes, I realize the very idea is ridiculous, but it shouldn't be. The mainstream is a hostile force seeking to demonize around half the population of America and we have grown used to it."

"With this latest information on the Club Q shooting the story has all but disappeared from the news feeds as if it never happened. Just like the Waukesha Massacre perpetrated by a BLM supporter, or the the alleged attack on Nancy Pelosi's husband, Paul Pelosi, and dozens of other recent crimes in which the facts do not serve the establishment narrative."

"What can we learn about leftists from the Club Q scenario in particular?"

"First, they are robotic in their responses rather than empathetic. They never pause to consider the complexities of the situation or wait to find out the truth. They jump to the conclusions they WISH were true, rather than seeking to learn more. Much like children."

"Second, though the vast majority of crime in the US is committed within Democrat controlled cities and states, the left only wants to highlight a certain type of crime – mass shootings by straight white males. These events serve their political interests while the others do not. You will not hear Democrats mention the high murder rate or black-on-black crime in anti-gun cities like Chicago, for instance. They don't care, because there's no benefits or power to be squeezed from that ongoing tragedy."

"Third, leftists are not interested in justice, they are interested in control. Justice is about punishing the people that actually committed the crime; but for them punishment of a suspect is secondary to the control that might be derived from the fear and panic the crime caused. Leftists will use any and every crisis or tragedy to demonize their political opponents."

"It's very difficult for the media to attach conservatives and the concept of hate crimes to a shooting enacted by a member of the gay community. Just as it was very difficult for them to attach white conservatives to hate crimes against Asians last year when most of the attacks were committed in heavily leftist cities by mostly black assailants."

"Fourth, leftists will happily stand on the bodies of victims to undermine rational conservative positions. In the aftermath of Club Q, there was a mass campaign to attack the conservative stance against the grooming of children in public schools and "all ages" drag shows. Leftists have decided for some reason that the sexualization of children is a hill they are willing to die on, and they will stop at nothing to justify drag dances and gender identity propaganda targeting kids."

"We can speculate on why Democrats are so obsessed with getting kids in front of dancing drag queens flashing their crotches, or forcing kids to use made-up identity pronouns while questioning their biology, but the simplest explanation is that they want to groom impressionable children into the leftist fold so that they can be controlled for the rest of their lives."

"It's not the LGBT part that we have a big problem with, it's the manipulation and targeting of children we have a problem with. Even if the Club Q shooter turned out to be a hardcore conservative instead of a trans person, that still wouldn't change the underlying situation. Two things can be true at the same time – Mass murder is wrong, and targeting children with political ideology and gender cultism is also wrong."

"Fifth, leftists often claim they have no interest in taking away American gun rights while at the same time demanding our guns be taken. It seems schizophrenic if you don't understand the concept of gaslighting, but narcissistic people often learn that saying one thing and doing the opposite is an excellent way to confuse their victims."

"As mentioned, they don't care about most crime in the US; they even try to deny rising crime statistics. However, they LOVE a mass shooting, especially the tiny percentage that involve military-style rifles, because they think it will give them the political capital needed to get a majority of people to support further gun restrictions or outright gun confiscation."

"It is a fact: Leftists want to end gun rights in the US regardless of the constitution. And, they are willing to punish ALL gun owners for the crimes of a handful of people. Again, this is not about justice, this is about control. Why do they want to take away gun rights if they don't actually care about the deaths of the people involved in crime? We can only conclude that a well armed population is a considerable obstacle to their agenda."

"The media will now have to play a game of spin as the Colorado shooting case unfolds. They are already claiming that the suspect is not actually trans, as if the suspect is faking as a means to avoid hate crime charges. If this is true, it would be a meaningless gesture as hate crime charges make no difference in the overall prosecution of multiple murders. Also, generally speaking, people who commit hate crimes would be loathe to identify as the thing they are supposed to hate."

"The fact remains that you cannot separate the political left from the tragedy-whoring and crisis opportunism they employ. Without constant calamity leftists serve no purpose and have no platform. They need disaster to remain relevant, and they need panic as a tool for centralizing power. They need the populace to be constantly afraid, mostly of threats that do not exist and suspicions that are misplaced."

"
They will attempt to gaslight and claim that conservatives are somehow the same – But we are not. We are not afraid of what we think they might do, we stand in opposition to what they are ALREADY doing. We aren't concerned about phantom enemies and imagined crises, we are concerned about the very real antagonists on our doorstep."

"This is one of the many differences between leftists and conservatives: We're not going to attack fellow Americans for things they have not done nor suspect people without evidence, we are only interested in stopping the trespasses that are happening right in front of our eyes. We aren't going to be victimized while our attackers pretend to be victims and we aren't going to pretend we don't see agendas that are obvious. Most of all, to the best of our ability we rely on the truth to make our case while leftists rely on deceit and spin."

"
The fact is, there is a divide now between leftists and conservatives that can never be mended. We are so different in our goals and our principles it is as if we are two different species, and for now only one side has acted consistently to destroy the other."

"We award a **Pinocchio rating of 8** to the violent left for their constant efforts to destroy the Constitution, wreak havoc and chaos in our life, destroy our cities and heritage, and attempt to disarm us."

Chuck Schumer (D-NY) Wants Amnesty for Millions of Illegal Aliens

Senate Majority Chuck Schumer (D-NY) suggests an amnesty for millions of illegal aliens eligible and enrolled in the Deferred Action for Childhood Arrivals (DACA) program is necessary to spike the United States population even as a record 331.9 million people reside in the U.S. Schumer stated "we have a population that is not reproducing on its own at the same level that it used to." Interestingly, the COVID jab is sterilizing our young and causing many pregnant women to abort! Isn't it ironic that all the illegal aliens are NOT being vaccinated. Plus the fact they are use to living in counties that have either socialistic or communistic regimes. What a perfect fit. All these illegals will make perfect democratic voters willing to work for low wages under a regime of strict censorship and not have to think. We bestow a **Pinocchio rating of 8.5** for Chuck Schumer's empathy for all these unvetted illegals; I believe the vatican will make him a saint for his humanitarian actions.

Dr. Fauci Caused 7 Million People To Die; "We've Caught Him Red Handed, He Won't Get Away"

Senator Rand Paul asserted Thursday that Anthony Fauci is directly responsible for funding dangerous gain of function research that likely killed millions of people, and that he "won't get away."

"Likely there is no public health figure who has made a greater error in judgement than Dr. Fauci," Paul declared in a Fox News appearance, adding "the error of judgement was to fund gain of function research in a totalitarian country."

Fauci funded "research that allowed them to create **super viruses,** that in all likelihood leaked into the public and caused seven million people to die."

A **Pinocchio rating of 10** is awarded to this mass murderer. Fauci makes Hitler look like a kindergarten teacher.

CDC Study confirms COVID Vaccination increases risk of suffering Autoimmune Disease affecting Heart by 13,200%

Myocarditis Cases Reported After mRNA-Based COVID-19 Vaccination in the US From December 2020 to August 2021
Matthew E. Oster, MD, MPH1,2,3; David K. Shay, MD, MPH1; John R. Su, MD, PhD, MPH1; et al. JAMA Jan. 25, 2022.

Covid Vaccines Part of Depopulation Agenda

If you listen to CNN, MSNBC, or any other mainstream media propaganda stations, they will tell you this is a conspiracy theory. For those not familiar with its origin, the term conspiracy theory was created by the CIA after the assassination of JFK to counteract all information that was contrary to the findings of the Warren Commission. In reality, a conspiracy theorist is one who does the research and makes up his or her's own mind based on the facts.

A recent documentary, "Died Suddenly," explains the alarming incidence of unexplained deaths around the globe over the past two years. Healthy adults are dropping dead all across the globe. In the last 18 months, the term 'Died Suddenly' has risen to the very top of 'most searched' Google terms." This is corroborated by the insurance companies putting out statistics showing the death rate is up by forty percent. Based on comments made by one expert, "this is the greatest orchestrated die-off in the history of the world."

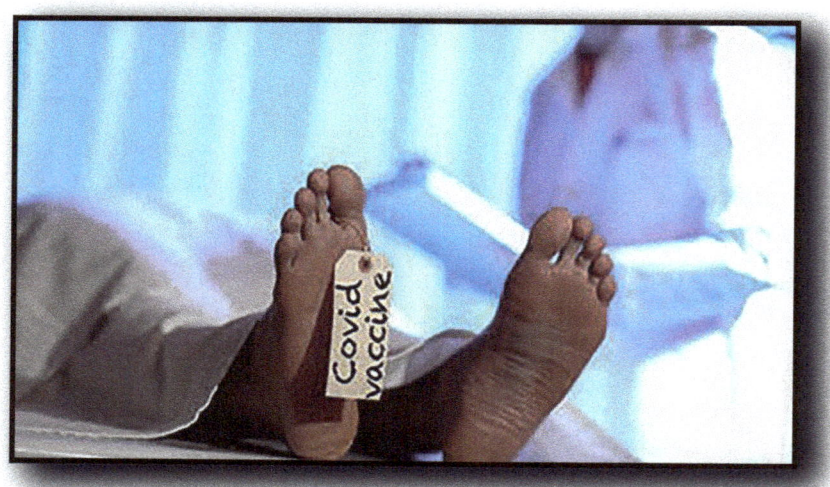

It would have been a lot worse if I didn't get the jab.

There is a very poignant statement on the top of one of the Georgia guide stones (https://www.youtube.com/watch?v=ixYqFQRjAs0) which states, "Maintain Humanity Under 500,000 in a Perpetual Balance with Nature - Guide Reproduction Wisely. I wonder what that means? A **Pinocchio rating of 10** is awarded for this diabolical experimental chemical for which there are no safety studies.

Who was Barry Seal?

Barry Seal was a contract pilot for the CIA flying guns to the Contras in Nicaragua and bringing cocaine back into the US landing in Mena, Arkinsas during the 1980s when Bill Clinton was Governor. The movie, American Made, was based on Barry Seal. Read the book, *Barry and the Boys* (by Daniel Hopsicker). Barry Seal was the biggest drug smuggler in American History and he was a CIA Agent.

While working as a drug smuggler and undercover informant for the CIA, during the Reagan administration, he photographed Pablo Escobar during one of his smuggling runs. Transcripts of court testimony show Seal allowed the CIA to equip the plane with hidden cameras that produced photographs of Nicaraguan government official Federico Vaughan loading a shipment of cocaine onto the C-123, with the help of members of the Cuban Army and reputed Colombian drug lord Pablo Escobar-Gaviria.

When the photographs were released to the press, Seal became a marked man. The official story was that Jorge Ochoa had murdered Seal in order to stop him from testifying at his U.S. trial. Yet Ochoa never stood trial in the U.S. Nor did Seal appear to be afraid of Ochoa. His concern was with George H. W. Bush and the CIA.

Speculation has long been that Seal was assassinated, not on cartel orders, but at the behest of the CIA. When Barry Seal was murdered, one of the items in his possession was his little black book, which had George W.H. Bush's private telephone number.

According to Sam Dalton, who was the New Orleans attorney who represented the Colombian hit men who killed Seal, "They [Barry Seal and George W.R. Bush] were regularly talking to each other very seriously over what was probably a secure phone," Dalton stated. "Barry Seal was in direct contact with George Bush."

Today, new sources like Sam Dalton are coming forward with forthright testimony to add to the voluminous evidence and testimony that already exists, testimony ranging from US Congressmen (former Ark. Rep. Bill Alexander) to state police (Arkansas State Criminal Investigator Russell Welch), to former drug pilots, that have testified that the CIA operation Barry Seal set up in Mena was used, and is still being used, to smuggle drugs with official sanction into the United States of America. A **Pinocchio rating of 10** is bestowed on this nefarious criminal along with George W.H.Bush, CIA, FBI, and all those associated with this gang.

Alder Berriman, or Barry Seal, was one of America's most notorious drug smugglers. He flew tons of cocaine and marijuana into the United States until he was busted in 1983 and became one of the DEA's most important informants.

According to The Real Raw News:
Nancy Pelosi, Other Deep Staters Arrested Following Biden's State Banquet

Article written by Michael Baxter -December 2, 2022

Karma and pay back: The proverbial shit is starting to hit the fan according to The Real Raw News. "United States Special Forces and Army Rangers on Thursday arrested Deep Staters—four politicians, two Hollywood actors, and two liberal media personalities–following the criminal Biden regime's gala extraordinaire banquet, where 300 black-tie guests feasted on taxpayer-funded Maine lobster, Almas caviar, and bottles of Chateau Margaux grand vin—at $200K per bottle."

"Contrary to the regime's narrative, the lavish celebration did not take place at the White House in Washington D.C.; rather, the deception took place at Tyler Perry's to-scale mockup of 1600 Pennsylvania Avenue, a precise facsimile of the real thing. Real Raw News and other alternative media have in the past elaborated on how the regime uses Perry's property to emulate official government functions."

USMC General David H. Berger along with 5th Special Forces Group Commander Brent Lindeman and 75th Ranger Regiment Commander Col. J.D. Keirsey were able to assist the 5th Special Forces Group Commander Brent Lindeman and 75th Ranger Regiment Commander Col. J.D. Keirsey to apprehend Nancy Pelosi and seven other Deep Staters. The names and charges will be released shortly. A **Pinocchio rating of 6** is assigned to the Deep Staters, Pelosi, and the other puppets who sold their souls. Idiots always believe that they will never be brought to justice.

"You can fool all the people some of the time and some of the people all the time, but you cannot fool all the people all the time." Abraham Lincoln (attributed to)

The Matrix Trilogy

Keanu Reeves stars as Thomas Anderson, known by his hacker alias "Neo," a computer programmer who has been searching for answers to cryptic messages about something called "the Matrix." He is contacted by a fellow hacker named Trinity (Carrie-Anne Moss), who speaks of a mysterious man called Morpheus (Laurence Fishburne) who will be able to give Neo the answers he has been looking for.

It has been said that Hollywood movies are used by the Deep State players to portray reality without the little people realizing it. By formatting these films as science fiction, they serve two purposes: one to entertain the masses; two they are showing the public exactly how they are enslaved within the matrix without actually realizing it. The best way to hide anything is to put it right in front of your face.

It's going to be hard for many to wrap their heads around this concept. For those with an opened mind, I strongly recommend you read the incredible works of Jon Rappoport, an investigative journalist. He has compiled over 1100 pages plus ten and a half hours of audio which make up the heart and soul of his Matrix Revealed. He has conducted interviews with the Matrix-insiders, who have first-hand knowledge of how the major illusions of our world are put together: Yes we are all living an illusion. Jon has 28 interviews with Ellis Medavoy, who is a master public relations expert and propagandist who worked for key controllers in the medical and political arenas who reveals how they pulled off the great deception. He also has 16 interviews with Richard Bell a financial analyst and trader who has a profound grasp of market manipulation and economic-rigging. The take-away information presented answers who is really running the world and how do they manufacture the illusion for the masses. The actual matrix we live in involves the government, money, energy, the military, the intelligence agencies, medicine, the mega corporations, psychology, mind control, and science. Rappoport's information transitions the science fiction into reality and how the elite players play the game and how the matrix was built. In the final analysis we have all been played. For many, they will not be able to handle the truth and they will continue to live the big lie. The choice is yours. A **Pinocchio rating of 10+** is bestowed on these manipulators who have twisted reality for their own benefit.

It's time to exit the Matrix.
How to Dismantle Society

The Marxist playbook spells it all out. First, you destroy the quality of the food. This

causes a deterioration of the health amongst the population. To day 60% of the US population has one major chronic illness. The COVID jab will bring this statistic to a much higher number. Second, destroy the children's identity. This is being carried out as we speak. Secretary of Education Miguel Cardona is the chosen one to carry out this transition from normalcy to non-binary children.

Army Cyber Command obtained disturbing, confidential letters Cardona authored and sent to school district superintendents in Arizona, California, Michigan, and New York. In the correspondence, Cardona brazenly encouraged districts to hire non-binary teachers, writing, "Modern youth must adopt the principles of a modern world, at an early age. Not every boy is a boy and not every girl is a girl. Exposure to non-binary faculty will help today's students—tomorrow's leaders—understand gender is a choice and not mandated at birth." Cardona's correspondence also mentioned hiring transvestites to increase diversity.

Cardona also sent school districts additional memos reaffirming his position that cisgender faculty be weeded out and replaced by staff espousing "progressive" values. In addition, Cardona promoted the notion that children as young as ten—4th graders—be taught about gender-reassignment surgery and puberty blockers, which prevent the development of organic, biological sex characteristics. Additionally, Cardona said he had petitioned HHS to pressure insurance companies to fund "gender-affirming care" for school kids. Cardona is pushing a radical agenda endangering the lives of children, exceeded his purview and must be held accountable.

Cardon's framework has nothing to do with education. It's indoctrination. It's corrupting the minds of malleable, impressionable children. He is guilty of treason against the country and against every child and parent in the country." Miguel has been given a **Pinocchio rating of 10** for his attempt to destroy our children's sexual identity.

How Easy it is to Make American Idiots Compliant

Henry Ford was once quoted as saying, "If you make people think they are thinking they will love you, but if you really make them think, they will hate you." A man dressed in sweats standing in front of an office building signals people walking in with his hand gesture to comply so he can apply a lint roller on them before allowing them to enter the building. Not one person objected. Now you know why our elections can easily be stollen, taxes raised without a fight, our southern borders remain open, and allow getting jabbed with an experimental chemical that has no track record. Interestingly, one cannot buy an automobile without it having a crash test to determine safety; one cannot buy an electric tool without it having been tested for safety, one cannot bring a newborn home from the hospital without verifying the safety of the car seat. Yet these medical idiots want you to take an experiment chemical that has no safety tract record. A Pinocchio rating of 4 is given to all those American idiots to who comply without thinking.

CLICK TO VIEW VIDEO

Pornographic Books in Their Children's School Libraries

When I went to school back in the 1950s, I would have been suspended for having a Playboy magazine in my possession. "Newspapers can't print pornographic material, and you'd be arrested if you gave it to a child on the street. So, why is this in our children's library?" The following article portrays this disturbing situation better than I can.

Jacob Asmussen | March 16, 2022

"As parents across the nation speak out against racist and pornographic material in children's schools, the fight is also occurring in communities across Texas."

"One of the latest examples is in the quaint and conservative hill country tourist town of Fredericksburg, located nearly two hours west of Austin, where parents like Tara Petsch have discovered pedophilia and explicit sexual acts and violence in books within their taxpayer-funded middle and high school libraries."

"What we have found are fictional novels depicting adult and child sex, normalizing pedophilia between teachers and students, incest, rape, graphic detailed sex scenes between minors, [and] sexual harassment language between characters who are minors and adults," Tara recently testified to the school board of the Fredericksburg Independent School District."

"Tara, a former teacher and school administrator from the Houston area, recently moved with her husband and their four kids to Fredericksburg to escape the craziness of the big city. She didn't expect to find this."

"These are not nonfiction sex education books; these pose no direct educational use. These are books that should be in an adult section of Barnes & Noble, but unfortunately, they're in our libraries," she said."

"Tara and a group of concerned parents started a website called MakeSchoolsSafeAgain.com, where they posted excerpts of explicit books found in FISD schools—including "Looking for Alaska," which details an oral sex scene between minors, and "Fade," which is about teachers using a date rape drug on students."

"Both books are available to children as young as 10 years old."

"There's a big difference in a parent challenging a book for political or religious reasons, and a parent challenging a library book that depicts adult teachers and children having sex," Tara told the school board at the recent public meeting."

"We've never asked for book banning. We've never asked for book burning. We've asked for book boundaries. We want age-appropriate books in our children's libraries. That's all we're asking," Tara told Texas Scorecard, adding, "Newspapers can't print this material, and you'd be arrested if you gave it to a child on the street. So, why is this in our children's library?"
"
Tara said she sent FISD administrators the book excerpts and is working with other parents to bring awareness to the community, especially because many people "just don't believe it's actually happening."

"When concerned parents brought this to the attention of principals and district administrators in FISD, we were told that we had to fill out forms and wait for a committee to read the entire book, and then it would be decided by you, the school board, if the books should be removed," Tara told the trustees. "We were also told that removing these pornographic books could be deemed as limiting a child's First Amendment right. And I can assure you that the law is on your side, and access to pornography is not a child's First Amendment right. To us, this is an urgent matter and it needs the school board's immediate attention."

"Tara explained to the board that one of their 2017 policies prohibits librarians from immediately removing obvious pornographic books."

This is another prime example of the moral decay that is infiltrating our society. We give the American idiots of the school boards a **Pinocchio rating of 8** for corrupting the morals of minors.

How Did The Deep State Set up the Maxtrix

The answer is simple but complex. They gained control of everything the sheeple are exposed to: Hollywood movies, which are a powerful means of setting trends, influencing behavior and beliefs, and instilling subliminal messages while you watch. No matter what talking head you listen to or what mainstream newspaper you read or radio station you listen to all these communication media outlets are controlled by six families. By catapulting young entertainers to stardom, the Deep State (DS) players now control and set the entertainment trends; rap pushes the agenda to kill police, burn down federal buildings, businesses, create riots, etc., etc. Big Pharma advertises which drugs, Nexium the purple pill, you should demand when you see your doctor. Wall Street creates phony investments, derivatives, to fleece the people. The congressmen and congresswomen are bought off and pass legislation that are not in your best interest and these scoundrels don't even have to worry about being re-elected because the voting machines, mail-in ballots, ballot harvesting, altered voting machine software and delayed counting of the ballots are means for rigging an election. It has also come to light that the FBI, DOJ and other governmental agencies were complicit in suppressing information, Hunter Biden's laptop, to influence voters. The central banking system has effectively enslaved the masses by putting people in debt: cars, houses, loan payments are every day examples how the average person pays triple the amount they borrow via the interest payments. The IRS, which is NOT a governmental agency, instills FEAR amongst the masses. The Federal Reserve Bank, which also is NOT a governmental agency, raises and lowers interest rates to create an economic rollercoaster ride and floods the market with monopoly money and even creates a depression periodically. The DS also instigates wars (like the one they are trying to start with Russia) to distract everyone's attention while you are being fleeced.

The DS also creates false flag events, Oklahoma bombing, World Trade Center attack to name a few, to conveniently take your freedoms (TSA agents at airports) away from you to make you safe.

Social media, Facebook, Twitter (before Elon Musk took over), TicTok are means of controlling public opinion using bots to give the illusion of consensus of current issues. The infiltration of our school systems from kindergarten to our colleges with crazy liberal teachers to indoctrinate our children. The CIA brings in hard core drugs (*Barry and the Boys*) to screw up peoples brains so they become ineffective citizens. Food manufacturers poison and degrade our food with synthetic vitamins, adulterated oils, processed, chemicalized foods, bleached flour and diet sodas to wreck our health while the medical establishment practices antiquated medicine.

How does the Deep State know when they have gained control of the masses. When the majority of the American idiots wear their hats backward and wear backpacks. Then they know they gotcha..The Deep State gets a **Pinocchio rating of 10+** for their actions to destroy our world.

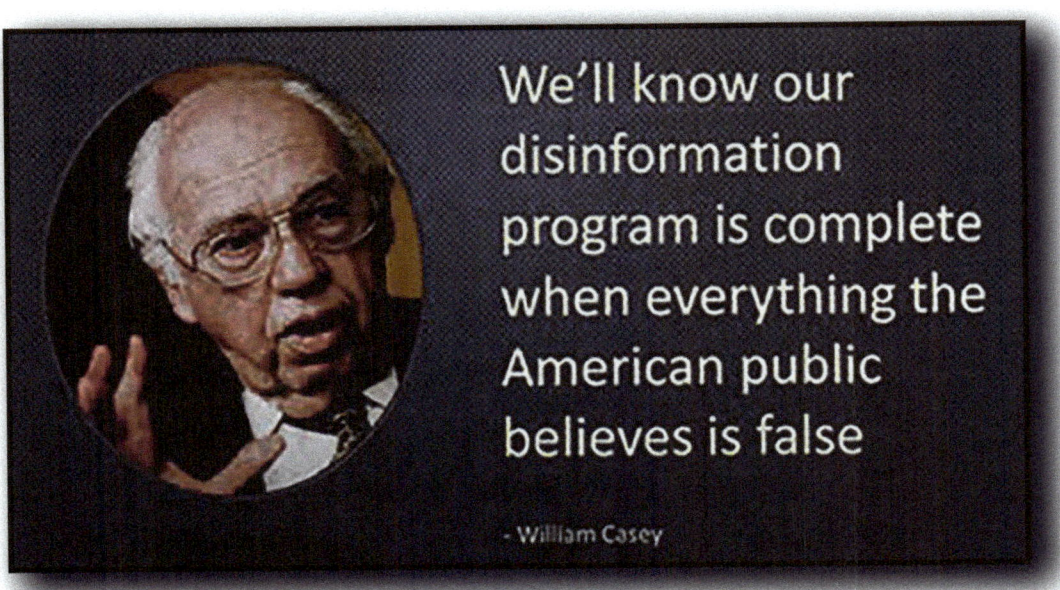

We'll know our disinformation program is complete when everything the American public believes is false

- William Casey

William Casey former CIA Director

How Patriots Can Push Back

Most teenagers today are comatosed but there are a few patriot teenagers that have the guts to stand up to the establishment. One such incident recently occurred in a Pennsylvania catholic school where a liberal oriented history teacher requested the students write an essay describing all the attributes of the Biden administration and all the bad policies of the Trump administration. The knowledgeable student who was very aware of current events and had a very conservative background left the classroom and reported the activity of this liberal teacher. Believe it or not, the liberal teacher was suspended. Chalk one up for the white hats. If people do not start to push back, it is all over for America and the world. Once America falls so goes the rest of humanity.

The propaganda machine has been turned against parents who have begun to push back against the Critical Race Theory being taught to their children. In an attempt to discredit parents who object to this brainwashing, the FBI now labels these awakened parents as domestic terrorists. We the People better start waking up to this Marxist playbook and nip it in the bud before we loose our country.

What the Obamas' $65 million book deal actually means

After Barack and Michelle Obama left the White House, they each sold a book in a joint deal that appears to be bigger than any previous presidential book deal in history. Reportedly, they are making $65 million, which is an unprecedented amount of money for a presidential memoir.

The Obamas are reportedly earning more than $65 million in this deal. That's way more than the Clintons got.

Penguin Random House, which bought the two books, won't discuss the numbers, but the Financial Times reports that the bidding for world rights surpassed $65 million. That number well exceeds the industry's already-lofty expectations about the Obamas' literary earning power. On the surface it appears to be a sweet deal. In reality, the American taxpayer paid the 65 million dollars plus. While Barack was president he gave Pearson Publishing, a subsidiary of Penguin Random House, a government contract worth $350 million for their work to create the Common Core textbook for his administration's education initiative. Do you think this was a gift from the publisher? The American people got fleeced again. We bestow the Pinocchio rating of 6 for this charade.

Two Block Busters: Michele Obama is a Man!
(Michael LaVon Robinson)

There are a lot of normies that won't believe it. Watch the video and make up your own mind. It has to be the biggest hoax ever pulled off in the history of civilization.

Larry Sinclair gives a press conference where he admits he did hard core drugs and had sex with then Senator Barack Obama

One month following Larry Sinclair's confession he was found dead. A Pinocchio rating of 10+ for these two American Idiots.

The Great American Give Away

California task force: Reparations for direct descendants of enslaved people only

California's first-in-the-nation task force to identify reparations for African Americans voted Tuesday to limit eligibility to those who can trace their lineage. Gavin Newsom's reparations committee will recommend handing out $223,200 per person to all descendants of slaves in California for 'housing discrimination' at a cost of $559 billion - in nation's biggest restitution effort ever. Maybe this will lower the number of people sleeping on the street. I aways said Gavin Newson was a genus.

California Governor Gavin Newsom signed legislation in 2020 launching the largest slavery reparations program in the country's history. I cannot wait until Gavin Newsom goes to Washington, DC. I bet he could fix the US deficit. Hands down Gavin gets our **Pinocchio rating of 10** and he will also receive a bonus get out of jail card plus $200 for passing go.

Calhoun's "Mouse Utopia" Experiments are now Coming True for Humanity as Self-Annihilation, Infanticide and Gender Distortions Become Commonplace
Mike Adams | NaturalNews.com

(Natural News) In the 1960's, a scientist named John Calhoun created a "mouse utopia" where populations of mice would enjoy everything they needed, essentially without effort: Unlimited food, water, living space, population growth without predators and so on. It started with eight mice, who began to reproduce quickly, enjoying their newfound "utopia" with unlimited resources. Within 4 years, however, the population had become extinct through self-annihilation even though all the resources it needed for survival were readily available, including ample space to live.

What happened to Calhoun's mice? He repeated the experiment multiple times using mice and rats. Each time the outcome was the same: Extinction within 1588 days. (Populations began to collapse at around 560 days, for reasons discussed below.)

What we are witnessing in the world today, right now, with the self-inflicted annihilation of humankind, almost perfectly reflects observations from Calhoun's "mouse utopia" experiments. Except now, it's happening in the world of humans.

Filmmaker Mike Freeman has even made a film about these experiments. It's called Critical Mass, and you can learn about it at CriticalMassFilm.com.

A bioethicist named Jan Kuba? has written extensively about this on a site called PhysicsOfLife.pl. There, on a page dedicated to Calhoun's experiment, he describes the Calhoun experiments as, "one of the most important in human history," and he delves into the meaning of all this for humankind. On this page, he describes the phases of live and annihilation through which the "mouse utopia" passed. Here's a summary:

Phase A – Day 1 – Strive period – Establishing territories and making nests. First children born.

Phase B – Day 105 – Exploit period – Rapid population growth. Social hierarchy established. Offspring higher in those with social dominance.

Phase C – Day 315 – Stagnation phase – Population growth slows. Males become feminized. Females become aggressive, taking over roles of males. Violence becomes common. Social disorder skyrockets. Male mice begin to assume female roles (mouse transgenderism). Mouse / rat homosexuality begins to emerge. Pedophilia grows rampant as "they begin mounting the young." Fertility falls in females. Mothers reject their young.

Phase D – Day 560 – Death phase – Population collapses. "No young surviving." No longer any conception. Non-reproducing females resort to eating, grooming and sleeping. No interest in socialization. No social skills learned by remaining survivors. No ability to be aggressive, which means no ability to defend their young or their nests. Avoidance of all stressful activities, including anything resembling competition. Preoccupation with grooming and physical attractiveness. Inability to navigate challenges of the real world. Only the outer appearance of being superior, but lacking cognitive and social skills. Totally unable to reproduce, raise young or compete for anything.

Utopia leads to extinction

As Kuban writes:

John Calhoun's collaborator's conclusions:

– The larger the population, the less care a mother gives to her nest and young.

Non-academic conclusions drawn by people educated in life:

– The principal factor is the lack of social education in the young

– Due to the abundance of food and water and lack of predators, there was no need to perform any actions to acquire resources and/or avoid danger. So the young have no opportunity to see such actions, learn (bad pupils often lose their lives) and, later, use them effectively.

– Utopia (when one has everything, at any moment, for no expenditure) declines responsibility, effectiveness and awareness of social dependence, and finally, as Dr Calhoun's study showed, leads to self-extinction.

– Contrarily, difficult conditions instigate better coping mechanisms for the population, leading to its growth, strengthening and reinforcement.

Lawrence W. Reed, writing for FEE.org, adds the following observation on all this in an article about the rise of the welfare state:

The turning point in this mouse utopia, Calhoun observed, occurred on Day 315 when the first signs appeared of a breakdown in social norms and structure. Aberrations included the following: females abandoning their young; males no longer defending their territory; and both sexes becoming more violent and aggressive. Deviant behavior, sexual and social, mounted with each passing day. The last thousand mice to be born tended to avoid stressful activity and focused their attention increasingly on themselves.

We are seeing the same thing in today's human societies
Many scientists have dismissed any link between Calhoun's "mouse utopia" experiments and human society, but in the years since these conclusions were drawn, human society has come to strikingly resemble the self-annihilation tendencies of the mice.

For example, in human society today, we note that socialism / progressivism teaches children that competition is bad. "Everyone's a winner" is the mantra of our time, and this creates an environment where children are not challenged. In fact, it is no longer even socially acceptable to subject children to any challenges at all. Students are selected into colleges merely based on their skin color or sexual orientations, and corporations hire people based on precisely the same traits, regardless of merit. As Kuban writes, the principle conclusion of Calhoun's experiments is as follows:

The lack of challenges gradually spoils the behavior
of subsequent generations of a population.

This degeneration is inevitable
and leads to eventual self-extinction.
Due to the lack of challenges, the extinction
of a population is inevitable.
It lasts several generations, but is inexorable.

This is precisely the path being pursued by left-wing socialism / communism / collectivism. This also highlights the dangers of a Universal Basic Income (UBI) or welfare / stimulus giveaways. When you give resources to populations without any apparent scarcity or competition, those population raise generations of offspring that are incapable of functioning in society.

We are seeing all the other signs of the mouse utopia collapse in modern human society as well:

– Infanticide and abortion, even the celebration of killing the young

– Rampant homosexuality and transgenderism

– Pedophilia and exploitation of the young by older members of society

– Increased violence

– Collapsing socialization skills, exacerbated by masks and lockdowns

– Obsession with self-grooming behaviors, as we see demonstrated by today's youth when it comes to selfies, social media presence, etc.

– Collapse in fertility of both males and females; spontaneous abortions, stillbirths, inability to cope with adversity

– Bullying of certain individuals in the population, withdrawal from social circles. If these mice had guns, there would have been mass mice shootings.

– Complete withdrawal from biological reproduction as transgenderism, pedophilia, violence and lunacy takes over.

Does any of that sound familiar? It sounds like every left-wing city in western society. What the mice demonstrated in the 1960s, left-wing humans are living out in the 2020s. The only real difference is that a generation of mice takes about 50 days to play out, while a generation of humans takes about 20 – 25 years.

In summary, population itself is not the problem. Collectivism and the welfare state is what will lead to humanity's self-annihilation.

As economist Thomas Sowell stated, "The welfare state shields people from the consequences of their own mistakes, allowing irresponsibility to continue and to flourish among ever wider circles of people."

Food abundance has made humanity weak, privileged and unable to rise to any real challenge

Part of the shock here is how easy food availability — and gluttony — has led to the weakening of the human race. Where food and other resources are readily available, children don't learn about competition, scarcity, skills, socialization or achievement. It is scarcity that results in learning and leadership, and without scarcity, there is only gluttony, apathy and collapse.

Notably, the mice never ran out of physical space. This wasn't an "overpopulation" problem per se. It was self-annihilation stemming from the collapse of the culture of the mice. They no longer valued competition, achievement or resources. They became lazy, apathetic, self-obsessed and distorted through what we would now label LGBTQ behaviors or collectivism tendencies, ultimately leading to the total collapse of any viability of offspring. Zero population was the inevitable result.

These mice were prisoners in a large physical structure where they were granted unlimited resources. Today, eight billion human beings are living in a prison planet which provides large amounts of food and free money, but where human culture and fertility are rapidly collapsing.

The End of Your Freedom and the End of America as We Know it

I never though in a million years I would be witnessing what is happening to our country. All the surveillance technology, facial recognition, your computer watching and listening to you, security cameras everywhere, etc., etc., that China initiated and beta tested is being rolled out in the US. It's here folks. Why do you think the Biden administration is pushing for electric cars. The reason is total control. If the Deep State (DS) doesn't like your political philosophy or the way you behave, they can shut your car down.

The final solution is being rolled out. One of the DS's ultimate objective is to force the American sheeple to accept the central banking system's digital currency. Once this occurs it is game over for you, your children, your family your friends and neighbors. The ATM machine in the photo says it ALL. If you still hate Trump after this two plus years of a shit show, your commitment to stupidity is impressive. God bless all the American Idiots.

Do you remember when Justin Trudeau, the PM of Canada enacted "Emergency" Powers to freeze the bank accounts of those protesting for freedom? That wasn't a one-off. Because the same thing can happen to us.

"Irreverent and hard hitting, American Idiots is an incredible masterpiece documenting the most corrupt period in American history. It's one of the best written documentaries that connect the dots transforming mainstream media's illusionary depiction of the chaotic events into truth and reality."

"American Idiots is insightful, factual, interspersed with political humor giving the reader a clear understanding of the moral breakdown of America. A must read for everyone who wants a bird's eye view of our tumultuous times."

Frank Cerami
Owner & Chief Marketing Strategist
Cerami Creative Marketing & Advertising

The End